Jane Addams

A LIFE OF COOPERATION

by Ann-Marie Kishel

Lerner Publications Company • Minneapolis

Photo Acknowledgments

The images in this book are used with the permission of: © North Wind Picture Archives, pp. 4, 10, 17, 18, 20; Jane Addams Memorial Collection (JAMC neg. 1635) Special Collections, University Library University of Illinois at Chicago, p. 6; Rockford College Archives, p. 7; Swarthmore College Peace Collection, p. 8; Archives and Special Collections on Women in Medicine, Drexel University College of Medicine, p. 9; Jane Addams Memorial Collection (JAMC neg. 140) Special Collections, University Library University of Illinois at Chicago, p. 12; Jane Addams Memorial Collection (JAMC neg. 113) Special Collections, University Library University of Illinois at Chicago, p. 13; © Brown Brothers, p. 14; Photography Collection, Miriam and Ira D. Wallach Division of Art, Prints and Photographs, The New York Public Library, Astor, Lenox and Tilden Foundations, p. 16; Jane Addams Memorial Collection (JAMC neg. 261) Special Collections, University Library University of Illinois at Chicago, p. 21; Jane Addams Memorial Collection (JAMC neg. 437) Special Collections, University Library University of Illinois at Chicago, p. 22; Library of Congress, pp. 23 (LC-DIG-ggbain-29988), 24 (LC-DIG-nclc-00918), 25 (LC-USZ62-111462); Jane Addams Memorial Collection (JAMC neg. 53) Special Collections, University Library University of Illinois at Chicago, p. 26.

Front Cover: © Brown Brothers.

Text copyright © 2007 by Lerner Publishing Group, Inc.

Lerner Publications Company
A division of Lerner Publishing Group, Inc.
241 First Avenue North
Minneapolis, MN 55401 U.S.A.

Website address: www.lernerbooks.com

Words in **bold type** are explained in a glossary on page 31.

Library of Congress Cataloging-in-Publication Data

Kishel, Ann-Marie.
    Jane Addams : a life of cooperation / by Ann-Marie Kishel.
        p.   cm. — (Pull ahead books)
    Includes index.
    ISBN-13: 978–0–8225–6382–2 (lib. bdg. : alk. paper)
    ISBN-10: 0–8225–6382–7 (lib. bdg. : alk. paper)
    1. Addams, Jane, 1860–1935–Juvenile literature. 2. Women social workers—United States–Biography–Juvenile literature. 3. Women social reformers—United States–Biography–Juvenile literature. I. Title. II. Series.
HV40.32.A33K57 2007
361.92–dc22   2006003451

Manufactured in the United States of America
2 – JR – 9/1/09

Table of Contents

Jane Addams

Growing Up

How could you help someone who has less money than you? Jane Addams wanted to help the poor. She knew she could help more people if she worked together with others. This **cooperation** made the lives of many people better.

Jane loved her father very much. He always cared for other people. He taught Jane to be honest and caring.

John Huy Addams, Jane's father

Jane holds an umbrella in her college class picture.

Jane's father also wanted her to be an **educated** person. After she finished high school, Jane went to college.

Jane's father died shortly after she finished college. Jane was very sad about his death.

Jane missed her father.

Jane studied at this medical school.

Jane knew she wanted to help people. She studied to become a doctor. But she changed her mind.

Neighbors gather to talk.

A Way to Help

Jane took a trip to Britain. She visited a **settlement house**. This is a house in a poor neighborhood. People who live in a settlement house work to help their neighbors. They try to make the neighborhood a better place.

Neighbors visited the settlement house for many reasons. Some took classes. Some talked about how to solve their problems.

Girls take a cooking class at a settlement house.

Boys help with construction.

Jane saw how the people in the settlement house helped their neighbors. She wanted to help too.

Hull-House

Hull-House

Jane decided to open her own
settlement house. She knew she could
do more if she had someone to help
her. Jane's friend, Ellen Gates Starr,
wanted to help. In 1889, Jane and
Ellen moved into a house in Chicago.
It was called Hull-House. It was in a
poor neighborhood.

This Italian family lived near Hull-House.

Many of Jane's neighbors were new
immigrants. They had just moved to
the United States from other countries.

Jane's neighbors often had to work
long hours. It was hard to make
enough money to pay the bills.

Everyone had to work.

A group meets at Hull-House.

Working Together

Jane and Ellen wanted all their neighbors to be healthy and safe. They needed more help to meet this goal. Many **volunteers** offered to help.

Jane and Ellen's neighbors could not pay for child care. A volunteer started a free day care.

Children attend day care at Hull-House.

Immigrants learn how to become U.S. citizens.

A volunteer worked with immigrants at
Hull-House. She taught them about
living in the United States.

A man offered Jane some old apartment buildings. Jane told him to tear them down. He built a playground where the buildings had been.

Children play on the playground near Hull-House.

Doctor Alice Hamilton cared for babies at Hull-House.

A doctor who volunteered at Hull-House gave checkups to babies. She also taught people how to stay healthy.

A volunteer worked with Jane to get laws passed. These laws said that women and children could work only eight hours a day.

Even young children had to work.

Julia Lathrop made sure children were treated fairly.

Another volunteer at Hull-House started the first **court** for children. Before this, children who broke laws were treated like adults.

Jane talks with a girl at Hull-House.

A Life of Cooperation

Jane Addams cared about people. She believed in helping others. Throughout her life, Jane cooperated with others to improve many people's lives.

JANE ADDAMS TIMELINE

1860
Jane Addams is born in Cedarville, Illinois, on September 6.

1888
Jane visits a settlement house in Britain.

1881
Jane graduates from college.

1889
Jane starts the Hull-House settlement house in Chicago.

1909

Jane helps create the National Association for the Advancement of Colored People (NAACP).

1931

Jane wins the Nobel Peace Prize.

1910

Jane writes a book called *Twenty Years At Hull-House*.

1935

Jane dies on May 21.

More about Jane Addams

● Jane Addams was the first American woman to win the Nobel Peace Prize. She won it in 1931 for her work trying to stop World War I.

● In 1909, Jane Addams helped start the NAACP. The NAACP defends the rights of blacks and all Americans.

● The only paying job Jane Addams ever had was as a garbage collector.

Websites

Jane Addams
http://www.americaslibrary.gov/cgi-bin/page.cgi/aa/activists/addams

Urban Experience in Chicago: Hull-House and Its Neighborhoods
http://www.uic.edu/jaddams/hull/urbanexp/

Glossary

cooperation: working together

court: a room or building in which legal cases are heard

educated: trained in school and knowledgeable about a wide variety of topics

immigrants: people who have moved to a new country

Nobel Peace Prize: an honor given for a person's work toward peace

settlement house: a place where people meet, get help, and have fun

volunteers: people who offer to help in some way, usually without pay

Index